This delightful book is the latest in the series of Ladybird books which have been specially planned to help grown-ups with the world about them.

As in the other books in this series, the large clear script, the careful choice of words, the frequent repetition and the thoughtful matching of text with pictures all enable grown-ups to think they have taught themselves to cope. The subject of the book will greatly appeal to grown-ups.

Series 999

THE LADYBIRD
BOOKS FOR GROWN-UPS SERIES

THE SICKIE

by

J.A. HAZELEY, N.S.F.W. and J.P. MORRIS, O.M.G.

(Authors of 'Breakdancing The Benedictine Way')

Publishers: Ladybird Books Ltd., Loughborough
Printed in England. If wet, Italy.

There are lots of reasons not to go to work.

Perhaps you are ill.

Or perhaps you are pretending to be ill so you can spend the day with your robots.

Henry is suffering from a mysterious but symptomless twenty–four–hour virus that can only be treated with fresh air.

He would not want any of his work colleagues to catch it, so he is staying as far away from them as possible.

Laurence and Ben are enjoying a bout of imaginary food poisoning.

Food poisoning is always good because it is over quickly and nobody likes to hear stories about toilets.

When Jesse gets home from a very big party, he phones his manager and leaves a message. Now he does not have to get up early to call in sick.

"Calling the office at 3.07am is exactly what someone with a real cold would do," Jesse thinks to himself as he falls asleep on his stairs with a kebab for a pillow.

A sickie will always seem more convincing if you can get a note from a doctor or the last rites from a priest.

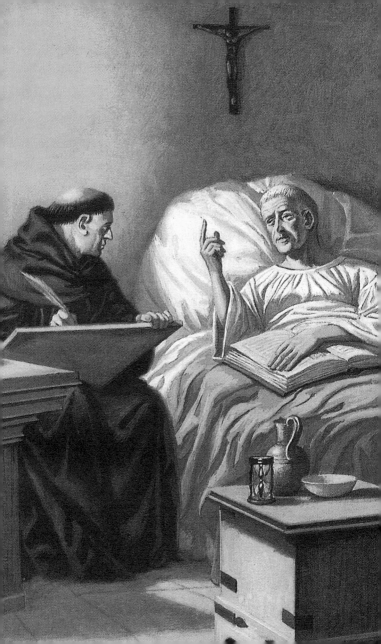

Gary has "had a cold coming on" all week at work.

Sniff. Sniff. Sniff. Sniff.

People are starting to suspect he is trying to get Friday off for a long weekend. Gary needs to up his game.

Gary's next sneeze is going to end in a frightening snapping noise.

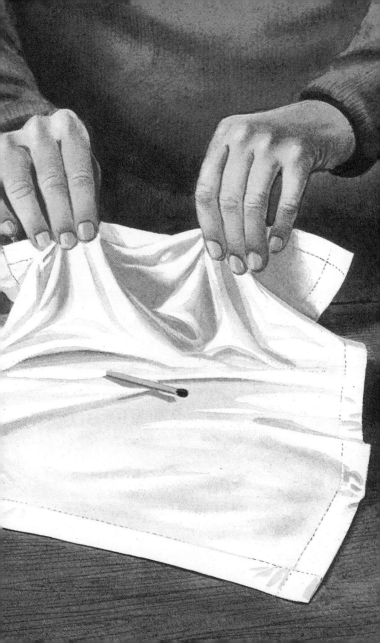

An apple a day keeps the doctor away.

But eating nothing but apples is a good way of inducing strategic diarrhoea.

Sacha cannot go to work today because she is sick.

She is particularly sick of Kizzy in the office going on about this new Danish mini-series about soaking-wet yachtsmen.

When Sacha has seen all twelve episodes, she will probably be well enough to go back to work.

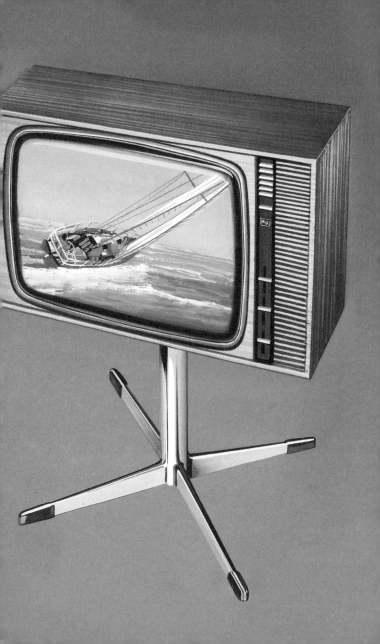

Gregor phones the office to tell them he cannot come in for his appraisal today because he has found himself transformed in his bed into a gigantic insect.

Gregor is frankly trying his luck.

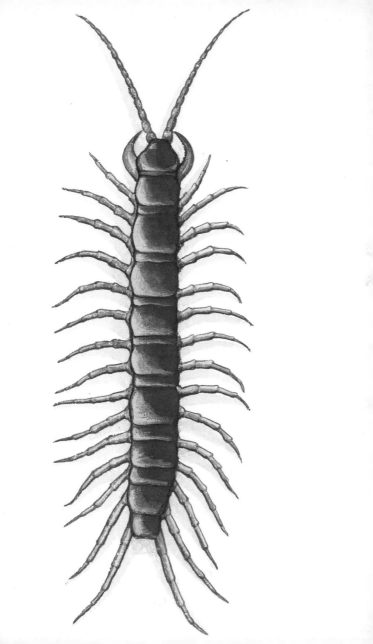

On 14th November 1939, British Naval Commander Sir Gideon Beauchamp sent a telegram to the Admiralty complaining of a dicky tummy.

Five years later, he was spotted celebrating V.E. Day in Trafalgar Square, court martialled and shot.

It remains the most successful sickie of the war.

Carrie's husband Mick has got so far into bed that she cannot find him.

"Come on, Mick. It's just a cold," says Carrie. "Where are you?"

The mattress coughs.

The boys are worried.

Uncle Tony has not moved for two hours.

He will make a miraculous recovery shortly after the Christmas washing—up has been done, and just in time for The Spy Who Loved Me.

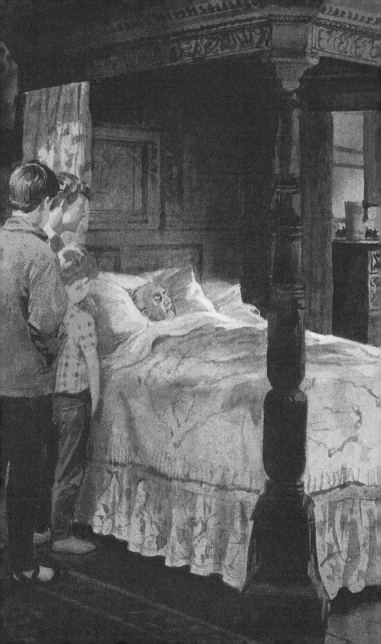

This state-of-the-art telephone processing centre is installed in the H.R. department of a national supermarket chain.

It can cope with sickie volumes of up to 40 calls per minute during the World Cup, Six Nations Rugby, or the first day it's really cold after the clocks go back.

So far, Ryan has been forced to miss a team—building day and a mindfulness seminar due to unexpected pen—knife injuries at work.

Ryan hopes that his firm does not schedule any other pointless wastes of his precious time because he is fast running out of ears.

Jemma had an essay to hand in this morning. She started it yesterday and managed one paragraph before giving up and watching Pointless.

Pointless is on again in a few hours.

Jemma is studying philosophy at Trinity College, but she might switch to media studies so she can justify staying in bed and watching so much Pointless.

Ghyslain has taken the day off work with a serious illness. He has a bad headache, listlessness, nausea, dizziness, dry mouth, feverish sweats and blotchy skin.

Ghyslain quietly gives thanks to Wikipedia that the symptoms of Lyme disease so conveniently match the symptoms of eleven pints of Belgian fruit cider.

Navin is having terrible trouble getting out of bed this morning.

Morgan spent the whole journey to the rock festival reading up the symptoms for norovirus in case his line manager phoned and asked where he was.

He has thought about norovirus so hard that he is now convinced he has norovirus.

Morgan has to admit that the hot sweats and hallucinations are spoiling Fleetwood Mac.

Charlie told his line manager he was going to the funeral of his Uncle Nigel when he was, in fact, watching the men's singles final at Wimbledon.

But, to his horror, he found out Uncle Nigel and his line manager are members of the same choir.

He is having to lure Uncle Nigel into the cellar, where he will be kept until Charlie can find a new job.

This term—time holiday was the only one David could afford.

David is not happy about training his boys to lie without blinking, or that they are missing out on their education, but maybe they can find careers as actors or politicians.

Her boss may have called her bluff, but Verna still counts this as one of her better sickies.

"It's at least a week off," she says to herself. "And I've always got the other kidney."

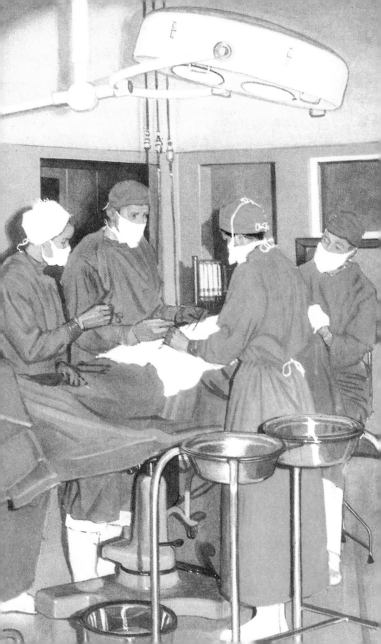

"Your dad says he can't take you to Jungle Climbers because he has rinderpest," reads Paula.

Rinderpest is a viral infection of cows and warthogs which was eradicated globally in 2001.

Paula says looking for where Dad is hiding will be nearly as much fun as Jungle Climbers.

Oomsk does not want to go on the bear hunt. He wants to stay tucked up in his furs, watching a new fire he's really into.

His wife Oomska does not believe he is sick. She has insisted on calling Elder Poobab and his healing sticks.

Oomsk is working out which made—up symptoms will not make Elder Poobab drill a hole in his head.

Simon has taken the day off because it is raining.

"Being rained on is technically an assault occasioning actual bodily harm," he says to his superior.

Simon loves being a barrister.

THE AUTHORS would like to record their gratitude and offer their apologies to the many Ladybird artists whose luminous work formed the glorious wallpaper of countless childhoods. Revisiting it for this book as grown-ups has been a privilege.

MICHAEL JOSEPH

UK | USA | Canada | Ireland | Australia
India | New Zealand | South Africa

Michael Joseph is part of the Penguin Random House group of companies whose addresses can be found at global.penguinrandomhouse.com

First published 2016
001

Printed in Italy by L.E.G.O. S.p.A

A CIP catalogue record for this book is available from the British Library

ISBN: 978–0–718–18443–8

www.greenpenguin.co.uk